POEMS OF TWO WARS

Poems of Two Wars

Laurence Binyon

Edited by Paul O'Prey

dark-pale

First published in Great Britain in 2016 by Dare-Gale Press

32 Loman Street,
London SE1 0EH

www.daregale.com

Poems © Laurence Binyon 1931, 1941, 1944, 1947
Introduction and this selection © Paul O'Prey 2016

Front cover: 'St Clement Dane's Church on Fire after being
Bombed', by Henry Carr. Reproduced by permission of the
Imperial War Museum.

Back cover: portrait of Laurence Binyon by William Strang.
Reproduced by permission of Bel Mooney.

ISBN   978-0-9933311-1-4

Printed and bound in Great Britain by SRP Ltd, Exeter

It was on this same day that I watched the battlefield, sinister with all the science of desolation, and heard the guns blankly echo about the flayed and barren hills. Barrenness and destruction triumphed there, as if men's one desire were to disnature earth, to blast the tree, choke the spring, shrivel the grass, and most of all to break, maim, blind, and utterly destroy the body into which their souls were born.

Laurence Binyon, For Dauntless France (1918)

CONTENTS

Laurence Binyon (right) with Sébastien
at *l'hôpital temporaire*, Arc-en-Barrois, 1915

Introduction

Every year, at the eleventh hour of the eleventh day of the eleventh month, people come together in towns and villages across Britain to remember the men and women who lost their lives in war. The Service of Remembrance typically has three solemn moments: a minute's silence, a bugler playing the Last Post, and four lines of poetry that summon a nation's sense of grief:

> They shall grow not old, as we that are left grow old:
> Age shall not weary them, nor the years condemn.
> At the going down of the sun and in the morning
> We will remember them.

These famous lines, from Laurence Binyon's poem 'For the Fallen', carry echoes of Shakespeare, the King James Bible and the Book of Common Prayer – texts with profound resonance in the tribal memory at a time of national crisis. The last line's unexpected shortening itself enacts the sudden loss of young men killed before their time. These lines have been engraved onto thousands of war memorials across the world. In 1921 Eric Gill carved them onto the stone entrance of the British Museum. In 1916 Edward Elgar set this and Binyon's other early war poems to music, in his choral work 'The Spirit of England'.

The success of this poem, or rather the success of its fourth quatrain, has overshadowed Binyon's other work to the extent that he is sometimes now misconceived as a 'one-poem poet'. Binyon's achievement is considerably greater than this single verse and his admirers have included fellow poets as diverse as WB Yeats, TS Eliot, John Masefield and Isaac Rosenberg.

Binyon was born in Lancaster in 1869, the son of an Anglican clergyman. The family subsequently moved to London, where he attended St Paul's School. Binyon was a scholarly boy whose nickname was 'the Bard', and in 1888 he won a scholarship to study Classics, or 'Greats', at Trinity College Oxford. As a student he won the Newdigate Prize for Poetry and saw his first volume of poems published, a collection with three friends called *Primavera*. It was reviewed in the *Pall-Mall Gazette* by Oscar Wilde, who advised undergraduates to read it during lectures and noted approvingly that Binyon was capable of catching 'the sweet echoes that sleep in the sonnets of Shakespeare.'

After Oxford Binyon joined the British Museum, where he was to work for the next forty years, rising to the post of Keeper of Prints and Drawings. His four-volume catalogue of the Museum's collection of British drawings is still in use today. He began to augment his meagre salary (about the same as 'an unsuccessful organ-grinder') by writing reviews, articles and books on art. He was to become a leading authority on William Blake and an early European expert on Chinese and Japanese art. His books, *Painting in the Far East* (1908) and *The Flight of the Dragon* (1911) broke new ground and earned him a public reputation.

Binyon made his name as a poet in the 1890s with a series of poems on urban life in contemporary London, including sympathetic portraits of everyday or marginal characters such as builders, road-menders, a convict just released from prison, and a rag-picker. By 1901 the young Arthur Ransome, author of *Swallows and Amazons*, had taken to loitering outside Binyon's house at night, just to see the lamps guttering and to imagine the great poems he might be writing.

When war broke out in August 1914 Binyon was horrified by the savagery unleashed on Belgian towns he knew well, having written a book on Flemish architecture and art. It was the fall of Mons, just three weeks into the war, that spurred him to write 'For the Fallen' while he was on holiday in Cornwall. It is an elegy for the loss of young men fighting overseas, though he could not have imagined then that the war was to claim so many.

Binyon was over-age for military service but he was determined to 'be made use of' in some way. He initially volunteered as a reserve in the County of London Regiment, and was put in charge of a machine-gun first in Holland Park and then in Woolwich, as part of the city's defence against air attack. In July 1915 he volunteered with the Red Cross, taking holiday and unpaid leave from the Museum to serve at the front as a medical orderly. He was sent to the 180-bed 'English hospital' established in a chateau at Arc-en-Barrois in the Haute Marne, forty miles from the fighting, where poet John Masefield and painter Henry Tonks also volunteered.

Binyon's job involved hard, dirty, physical work, carrying patients, equipment and stores, and 'disposing of the pails of slops and dressings.' He assisted the surgeon during operations and afterwards incinerated the arms and legs that had been amputated. He rode in the ambulance to collect casualties, a task described vividly in one of his most evocative poems, 'Fetching the Wounded'. Amid the devastation Binyon found a fulfilling role for himself, assisting the doctors and nurses, and helping the 'heroic wounded'. He made many friends, including Sébastien, 'a Breton lad' with 'a roguish laugh' who hated the war but who remained optimistic, despite having lost a hand.

Direct experience of 'the misery, the wasting and maiming' meant Binyon's poems about the war changed radically. He no longer looked to Shakespeare or the Bible to help him express his feelings, but drew on his own experience:

> chaos, torture, blood,
> fire, thunder, and stench;
> And the savage shattering noise
> Of churned and shaken trench.

In 1917 the British Red Cross commissioned Binyon to write an account of their activities, which was to become a remarkable book, *For Dauntless France,* published in 1918. He spent a month touring French battlefields and hospitals, 'scenes of hideous slaughter and indescribable valour.' This commission afforded him a perspective on the war that was unique among poets at the front. He described his journey through 'an insane landscape, smelling of evil', a world denatured and dehumanised by modern industrial warfare:

> The landscape was, so to say, extinct. It had lost
> all its native life. The ground seemed inert, like
> the body of a dead creature under the claws
> of a fierce beast that shakes it now and then. It
> had convulsions of movement, not its own [...]
> Men, as men, appeared no longer to exist.

Binyon was one of fifty writers who signed a letter to *The Times* in September 1914 saying that 'Great Britain could not without dishonour have refused to take part in the present war.' By 1918, however, he shared in a wider disillusion, felt by Wilfred Owen and a great many others, that the world had little to show for its loss, that civilisation had grown 'deadened' through its acceptance of gross acts of inhumanity. In poems like 'Wingless Victory' and 'There is Still Splendour' he speaks bitterly of a catastrophic loss of values, and a betrayal of those who had died.

In 1933, aged 64, Binyon retired from the British Museum and succeeded TS Eliot as the Norton Professor of Poetry at Harvard University. Remarkably it was from this point on that Binyon wrote much of his best poetry. The onset of age and the approach of another war triggered a period of deep reflection and renewed creativity in him. His later poetry takes on a greater energy as well as a new sense of urgency and freedom. The poems he wrote during the Second World War are more personal and direct than anything that came before.

Binyon was a gentle, modest man, scholarly yet sociable, with a gift for friendship. Ezra Pound looked to him for guidance on Chinese art and found him to be 'one of the best-loved men in London' (he appears in Pound's *Cantos* as 'BinBin'). Cyril Connolly described him as 'a wise, poor, happy and incorruptible lover of truth and beauty… both warm and detached, in fact a sage.'

Binyon was self-effacing in both his life and art and in 1996 the poet Mick Imlah suggested that such a temperament 'must be judged in the end to have been inimical to the production of great poems.' Binyon's friend, Manmohan Ghose, told him while they were at Oxford together that the great flaw in his character and in his poems was that he was 'too perfect, too reasonable, too sinless'. Binyon expressed none of the anxiety and alienation on which modern tastes feed. As George Russell said of James Joyce, for a writer he seems not to have had enough chaos in him.

Binyon's positive nature finds its greatest expression in his love poems and in an almost mystical connection with the natural world, in passages that demand release from the constraints of tradition and formality. Here, in 'The Idols', he marvels as the various forms of life awaken in the dawn:

> I see them, I know them, I name them, I share in
> their being;
> I am not betrayed:
> I feel in my fibre the touch of a spirit that knows me;
> For this was I made.

His main weakness was perhaps to write, or rather to publish, too much. In 1931 Macmillan brought out his *Collected Poems*, a monumental 700 pages of poetry in two heavy volumes which did not include his several verse plays. There were two more volumes of poetry and another verse play to come. TS Eliot tried to lure Binyon to Faber where he was a director, with the offer of a more accessible *Selected Poems*, but permission was withheld by Macmillan. The company promised to bring out a selected poems of their own but never did, an omission that was to limit Binyon's potential readership. A sensitive pruning of the work by the discerning Eliot might have had a radical influence on Binyon's later reception.

If Binyon did indeed have insufficient chaos inside to create great confessional poems, he found plenty of chaos in the outside world to unsettle him. His direct experience of war on the Western Front and the Blitz in London produced poems of thoughtful witness, in which outrage sometimes borders on despair. The First World War and the Second World War were the two defining public events of his life and of his poetry and for this reason they provide the structure of the present volume, which is the first selection of Binyon's poems to be made based on the full body of his work.

His belief in the goodness of humanity was broken by the savagery he saw and touched for himself in the aftermath of the Battle of Verdun. During his tour of France for the Red Cross he felt 'a sort of humiliation at coming on this scene as a spectator' and he expresses a profound admiration for the fortitude and courage of the young men caught up in the fighting. There was no obligation on him to give up a comfortable life to go to France in 1915 and put himself through the bleakest of experiences, but he had a remarkably selfless sense of duty which gives his poetry of witness an authenticity that can stand alongside that of poets who played a direct part in the fighting.

When war broke out in 1939, Binyon (aged 70) again hoped to be made use of in some way and the following year he responded readily to a request from the British Council to go to Greece for four months as the Byron Professor of English Literature. He and his family had moved out of London before the war, but he saw for himself the effect of the Blitz, which led him to write his finest poem, 'The Burning of the Leaves', in 1942. This was published in *Horizon*, whose editor, Cyril Connolly, later thought it the finest single poem ever to be printed by the magazine. A reviewer in the *New Statesman and Nation* observed that Binyon 'wrote one of the best poems of the last war, and [...] one of the best poems in this.'

'The Burning of the Leaves' is a very different poem to 'For the Fallen' and shows how far Binyon had travelled both in terms of his creativity and his personal philosophy. Binyon's biographer, John Hatcher, points to the strong influence in the poem of Chinese classical philosophy and the works of Lao Tzu in particular. Binyon had written about the water imagery of the *Tao Te Ching*, with its 'secret of fluidity, of aspiring to pervade rather than to resist, to flow rather than to strive.' This is the unstoppable water that in the poem springs up amid the bombed ruins, which cannot be contained and which flows through the man-destroyed world bringing new life. This acceptance of life, with its elements of both darkness and light, of both the healing water and the destroying fire, creates a very different tone to the more conventional defiance of 'For the Fallen'.

'The Burning of the Leaves' is not a poem to be read aloud in church, nor will it be carved onto any war memorial. It is too mysterious, too mystical and too ambiguous for that. It is a poem of private rather than public consolation, accepting its own existential ambivalence, while rejecting the public world's easy answers. Standing amid ruins 'empty as a skull', the poet contemplates man's 'ecstasy of hate' and finds hope in a world stripped bare, a world reduced to the purest elements of fire, light and water, as the Earth again puts forth 'the leaf and the flower' that 'know not the lust of destruction, the frenzy of spite.'

The resilience of nature, and man's enduring trust

in and dependence on the natural world, is a constant theme in Binyon's poetry, a source of both consolation and redemption. Amidst the chaos and destruction he witnessed in France during the First World War, he was struck by the sight of a farmer sowing seed, who with 'a quick, deliberate toss' re-enacts 'the immemorial gesture of Man' putting his confidence in a summer harvest ('The Sower'). Many years later, as the world tore itself apart in another war, Binyon returns to this image in 'Sowing Seed'. Here the world is 'A thing to weep for, /Ripe for burial, /Veined with despair.' What saves the poet from this despair is an intuitive trust in the Earth and its rhythms of death and life, a 'trust that is deeper / Than fear can fathom /Or hope desert.'

When Binyon died in 1943 he was working on a poem, 'Winter Sunrise', and a verse play, 'The Madness of Merlin'. Neither are finished but I have included them here because they show Binyon at work and still at the height of his powers. Although 'Winter Sunrise' is clearly only a draft, Mick Imlah felt that 'it is perfect as it was left: the last of a thousand pages of verse, and miraculously the finest.' It is the final testament of a poet who chronicled the two world wars of the twentieth century with humanity, compassion and humility, but who also nurtured a spirit above war.

Paul O'Prey

The First War

Strange Fruit

This year the grain is heavy-ripe;
The apple shows a ruddier stripe;
Never berries so profuse
Blackened with so sweet a juice
On brambly hedges, summer-dyed.
The yellow leaves begin to glide;
But Earth in careless lap-ful treasures
Pledge of over-brimming measures,
As if some rich unwonted zest
Stirred prodigal within her breast.
And now, while plenty's left uncared,
The fruit unplucked, the sickle spared,
Where men go forth to waste and spill,
Toiling to burn, destroy and kill,
Lo, also side by side with these
Beast-hungers, ravening miseries,
The heart of man has brought to birth
Splendours richer than his earth.
Now in the thunder-hour of fate
Each one is kinder to his mate;
The surly smile; the hard forbear;
There's help and hope for all to share;
And sudden visions of goodwill
Transcending all the scope of ill
Like a glory of rare weather
Link us in common light together,
A clearness of the cleansing sun,
Where none's alone and all are one;
And touching each a priceless pain
We find our own true hearts again.
No more the easy masks deceive:
We give, we dare, and we believe.

The Harvest

Red-reapers under these sad August skies,
Proud War-Lords, careless of ten thousand dead,
Who leave earth's kindly crops unharvested
As you have left the kindness of the wise
For brutal menace and for clumsy lies,
The spawn of insolence by bragging fed,
With power and fraud in faith's and honour's stead,
Accounting these but good stupidities;

You reap a heavier harvest than you know.
Disnaturing a nation, you have thieved
Her name, her patient genius, while you thought
To fool the world and master it. You sought
Reality. It comes in hate and woe.
In the end you also shall not be deceived.

For the Fallen

With proud thanksgiving, a mother for her children,
England mourns for her dead across the sea.
Flesh of her flesh they were, spirit of her spirit,
Fallen in the cause of the free.

Solemn the drums thrill: Death august and royal
Sings sorrow up into immortal spheres.
There is music in the midst of desolation
And a glory that shines upon our tears.

They went with songs to the battle, they were young,
Straight of limb, true of eye, steady and aglow.
They were staunch to the end against odds uncounted,
They fell with their faces to the foe.

They shall grow not old, as we that are left grow old:
Age shall not weary them, nor the years condemn.
At the going down of the sun and in the morning
We will remember them.

They mingle not with their laughing comrades again;
They sit no more at familiar tables of home;
They have no lot in our labour of the day-time;
They sleep beyond England's foam.

But where our desires are and our hopes profound,
Felt as a well-spring that is hidden from sight,
To the innermost heart of their own land they are known
As the stars are known to the Night;

As the stars that shall be bright when we are dust,

Moving in marches upon the heavenly plain,
As the stars that are starry in the time of our darkness,
To the end, to the end, they remain.

Ode for September (excerpt)

Around a planet rolls the drum's alarm.
Far where the summer smiles
Upon the utmost isles,
Danger is treading silent as a fever-breath.
Now in the North the secret waters arm;
Under the wave is Death:
They fight in the very air, the virgin air,
Hovering on fierce wings to the onset: there
Nations to battle stream;
Earth smokes and cities burn;
Heaven thickens in a storm of shells that scream;
The long lines shattering break, turn and again return;
And still across a continent they teem,
Moving in myriads; more
Than ranks of flesh and blood, but soul with soul at war!

★

Now will we speak, while we have eyes for tears
And fibres to be wrung
And in our mouths a tongue.
We will bear wrongs untold but will not only bear;
Not only bear, but build through striving years
The answer of our prayer,
That whosoever has the noble name
Of man, shall not be yoked to alien shame;
That life shall be indeed
Life, not permitted breath
Of spirits wrenched and forced to others' need,
Robbed of their nature's joy and free alone in death.
The world shall travail in that cause, shall bleed,
But deep in hope it dwells
Until the morning break which the long night foretells.

The Anvil

Burned from the ore's rejected dross
The iron whitens in the heat.
With plangent strokes of pain and loss
The hammers on the iron beat.
Searched by the fire, through death and dole
We feel the iron in our soul.

O dreadful Forge! if torn and bruised
The heart, more urgent comes our cry
Not to be spared but to be used,
Brain, sinew and spirit, before we die.
Beat out the iron, edge it keen,
And shape us to the end we mean!

The Healers

In a vision of the night I saw them,
In the battles of the night.
'Mid the roar and the reeling shadows of blood
They were moving like light,

Light of the reason, guarded
Tense within the will,
As a lantern under a tossing of boughs
Burns steady and still.

With scrutiny calm, and with fingers
Patient as swift
They bind up the hurts and the pain-writhen
Bodies uplift,

Untired and defenceless; around them
With shrieks in its breath
Bursts stark from the terrible horizon
Impersonal death;

But they take not their courage from anger
That blinds the hot being;
They take not their pity from weakness;
Tender, yet seeing;

Feeling, yet nerved to the uttermost;
Keen, like steel;
Yet the wounds of the mind they are stricken with,
Who shall heal?

They endure to have eyes of the watcher

In hell, and not swerve
For an hour from the faith that they follow,
The light that they serve.

Man true to man, to his kindness
That overflows all,
To his spirit erect in the thunder
When all his forts fall, –

This light, in the tiger-mad welter
They serve and they save.
What song shall be worthy to sing of them –
Braver than the brave?

The Zeppelin

Guns! far and near,
Quick, sudden, angry,
They startle the still street.
Upturned faces appear,
Doors open on darkness,
There is a hurrying of feet,

And whirled athwart gloom
White fingers of alarm
Point at last there
Where illumined and dumb
A shape suspended
Hovers, a demon of the starry air!

Strange and cold as a dream
Of sinister fancy,
It charms like a snake,
Poised deadly in the gleam,
While bright explosions
Leap up to it and break.

Is it terror you seek
To exult in? Know then
Hearts are here
That the plunging beak
Of night-winged Havoc
Strikes not with fear

So much as it strings
To a deep elation
And a quivering pride

That at last the hour brings
For them too the danger
Of those who died,

Of those who yet fight
Spending for each of us
Their glorious blood
In the foreign night, –
That now we are neared to them
Thank we God.

Fetching the Wounded

At the road's end glimmer the station lights;
How small beneath the immense hollow of Night's
Lonely and living silence! Air that raced
And tingled on the eyelids as we faced
The long road stretched between the poplars flying
To the dark behind us, shuddering and sighing
With phantom foliage, lapses into hush.
Magical supersession! The loud rush
Swims into quiet: midnight reassumes
Its solitude; there's nothing but great glooms,
Blurred stars; whispering gusts; the hum of wires.
And swerving leftwards upon noiseless tires
We glide over the grass that smells of dew.
A wave of wonder bathes my body through!
For there in the headlamps' gloom-surrounded beam
Tall flowers spring before us, like a dream,
Each luminous little green leaf intimate
And motionless, distinct and delicate
With powdery white bloom fresh upon the stem,
As if that clear beam had created them
Out of the darkness. Never so intense
I felt the pang of beauty's innocence,
Earthly and yet unearthly.

       A sudden call!
We leap to ground, and I forget it all.
Each hurries on his errand; lanterns swing;
Dark shapes cross and re-cross the rails; we bring
Stretchers, and pile and number them; and heap
The blankets ready. Then we wait and keep
A listening ear. Nothing comes yet; all's still.

Only soft gusts upon the wires blow shrill
Fitfully, with a gentle spot of rain.
Then, ere one knows it, the long gradual train
Creeps quietly in and slowly stops. No sound
But a few voices' interchange. Around
Is the immense night-stillness, the expanse
Of faint stars over all the wounds of France.

Now stale odour of blood mingles with keen
Pure smell of grass and dew. Now lantern-sheen
Falls on brown faces opening patient eyes
And lips of gentle answers, where each lies
Supine upon his stretcher, black of beard
Or with young cheeks; on caps and tunics smeared
And stained, white bandages round foot or head
Or arm, discoloured here and there with red.
Sons of all corners of wide France; from Lille,
Douay, the land beneath the invader's heel,
Champagne, Touraine, the fisher-villages
Of Brittany, the valleyed Pyrenees,
Blue coasts of the South, old Paris streets. Argonne
Of ever smouldering battle, that anon
Leaps furious, brothered them in arms. They fell
In the trenched forest scarred with reeking shell.
Now strange the sound comes round them in the night
Of English voices. By the wavering light
Quickly we have borne them, one by one, to the air,
And sweating in the dark lift up with care,
Tense-sinewed, each to his place. The cars at last
Complete their burden: slowly, and then fast
We glide away.

      And the dim round of sky,
Infinite and silent, broods unseeingly

Over the shadowy uplands rolling black
Into far woods, and the long road we track
Bordered with apparitions, as we pass,
Of trembling poplars and lamp-whitened grass,
A brief procession flitting like a thought
Through a brain drowsing into slumber; nought
But we awake in the solitude immense!
But hurting the vague dumbness of my sense
Are fancies wandering the night: there steals
Into my heart, like something that one feels
In darkness, the still presence of far homes
Lost in deep country, and in little rooms
The vacant bed. I touch the world of pain
That is so silent. Then I see again
Only those infinitely patient faces
In the lantern beam, beneath the night's vast spaces,
Amid the shadows and the scented dew;
And those illumined flowers, springing anew
In freshness like a smile of secrecy
From the gloom-buried earth, return to me.
The village sleeps; blank walls, and windows barred.
But lights are moving in the hushed courtyard
As we glide up to the open door. The Chief
Gives every man his order, prompt and brief.
We carry up our wounded, one by one.
The first cock crows: the morrow is begun.

The Ebb of War

In the seven-times taken and re-taken town
Peace! The mind stops; sense argues against sense.
The August sun is ghostly in the street
As if the Silence of a thousand years
Were its familiar. All is as it was
At the instant of the shattering: flat-thrown walls;
Dislocated rafters; lintels blown awry
And toppling over; what were windows, mere
Gapings on mounds of dust and shapelessness;
Charred posts caught in a bramble of twisted iron;
Wires sagging tangled across the street; the black
Skeleton of a vine, wrenched from the old house
It clung to; a limp bell-pull; here and there
Little printed papers pasted on the wall.
It is like a madness crumpled up in stone,
Laughterless, tearless, meaningless; a frenzy
Stilled, like at ebb the shingle in sea-caves
Where the imagined weight of water swung
Its senseless crash with pebbles in myriads churned
By the random seethe. But here was flesh and blood,
Seeing eyes, feeling nerves; memoried minds
With the habit of the picture of these fields
And the white roads crossing the wide green plain,
All vanished! One could fancy the very fields
Were memory's projection, phantoms! All
Silent! The stone is hot to the touching hand.
Footsteps come strange to the sense. In the sloped
        churchyard,
Where the tower shows the blue through its great rents,
Shadow falls over pitiful wrecked graves,
And on the gravel a bare-headed boy,

Hands in his pockets, with large absent eyes,
Whistles the Marseillaise: To Arms, To Arms!
There is no other sound in the bright air.
It is as if they heard under the grass,
The dead men of the Marne, and their thin voice
Used those young lips to sing it from their graves,
The song that sang a nation into arms.
And far away to the listening ear in the silence
Like remote thunder throb the guns of France.

The Distant Guns

Negligently the cart-track descends into the valley;
The drench of the rain has passed and the clover
      breathes;
Scents are abroad; in the valley a mist whitens
Along the hidden river, where the evening smiles.
The trees are asleep, their shadows are longer and longer,
Melting blue in the tender twilight; above,
In a pallor, barred with lilac and ashen cloud,
Delicate as a spirit the young moon brightens,
And distant a bell intones the hour of peace,
Where roofs of the village, gray and red, cluster
In leafy dimness. Peace, old as the world!
The crickets shrilling in the high wet grass,
And gnats, clouding upon the frail wild roses,
Murmur of you: but hark! like a shudder upon the air,
Ominous and alien, knocking on the farther hills
As with airy hammers, the ghosts of terrible sound, –
Guns! From afar they are knocking on human hearts
Everywhere over the silent evening country,
Knocking with fear and dark presentiment. Only
The moon's beauty, where no life nor joy is,
Brightening softly and knowing nothing, has peace.

Men of Verdun

There are five men in the moonlight
That by their shadows stand:
Three hobble humped on crutches,
And two lack each a hand.

Frogs somewhere near the roadside
Chorus a chant absorbed;
But a hush breathes out of the dream-light
That far in heaven is orbed.

It is gentle as sleep falling
And wide as thought can span,
The ancient peace and wonder
That brims the heart of man.

Beyond the hills it shines now
On no peace but the dead,
On reek of trenches thunder-shocked,
Tense fury of wills in wrestle locked,
A chaos crumbled red!

The five men in the moonlight
Chat, joke, or gaze apart.
They talk of days and comrades;
But each one hides his heart.

They wear clean cap and tunic,
As when they went to war.
A gleam comes where the medal's pinned:
But they will fight no more.

The shadows, maimed and antic,
Gesture and shape distort,
Like mockery of a demon dumb
Out of the hell-din whence they come
That dogs them for his sport.

But as if dead men were risen
And stood before me there
With a terrible flame about them blown
In beams of spectral air,

I see them, men transfigured
As in a dream, dilate
Fabulous with the Titan-throb
Of battling Europe's fate;

For history's hushed before them,
And legend flames afresh.
Verdun, the name of thunder,
Is written on their flesh.

La Patrie

Through storm-blown gloom the subtle light persists;
Shapes of tumultuous, ghostly cloud appear,
Trailing a dark shower from hill-drenching mists:
Dawn, desolate in its majesty, is here.

But ere the wayside trees show leaf and form
Invisible larks in all the air around
Ripple their songs up through the gloom and storm,
As if the baulked light had won wings of sound!

A wounded soldier on his stretcher waits
His turn for the ambulance, by the glimmering rails;
He is wrapped in a rough brown blanket, like his mates:
Over him the dawn broadens, the cloud pales.

Muscular, swart, bearded, and quite still,
He lies, too tired to think, to wonder. Drops
From a leaf fall by him. For spent nerve and will
The world of shattering and stunned effort stops.

He feels the air, song-thrilled and fresh and dim
And close about him smells the rainy soil.
It is ever-living Earth recovers him,
Friend and companion of old, fruitful toil.

He is patient with her patience. Hurt, he takes
Strength from her rooted, still tenacities.
The will to heal, that secretly re-makes,
Like slumber, holds his dark, contented eyes.

For she, though – never reckoning of the cost –
Full germs of all profusion she prepares,

Knows tragic hours, too, parching famine, frost,
And wreck; and in her children's hurt she shares.

Build what we may, house us in lofty mind's
Palaces, wean the fine-wrought spirit apart,
Earth touches where the fibre throbs, and winds
The threads about us of her infinite heart.

And some dear ground with its own changing sky,
As if it were our feeling flesh, is wrought
Into the very body's dignity
And private colour of least conscious thought.

O when that loud invader burned and bruised
This ordered land's old kindness, with brute blows
Shamed and befouled and plundered and abused,
Was it not Earth that in her soldier rose

And armed him, terrible and simple? He
Takes his wound, mute as Earth is, yet as strong. –
The funeral clouds trail, wet wind shakes the tree,
But all the wild air of the dawn is song.

The Sower
(Eastern France)

Familiar, year by year, to the creaking wain
Is the long road's level ridge above the plain.
To-day a battery comes with horses and guns
On the straight road, that under the poplars runs,
At leisurely pace, the guns with mouths declined,
Harness merrily ringing, and dust behind.
Makers of widows, makers of orphans, they
Pass to their burial business, alert and gay.

But down in the field, where sun has the furrow dried,
Is a man who walks in the furrow with even stride.
At every step, with elbow jerked across,
He scatters seed in a quick, deliberate toss,
The immemorial gesture of Man confiding
To Earth, that restores tenfold in a season's gliding.
He is grave and patient, sowing his children's bread:
He treads the kindly furrow, nor turns his head.

Guns at the Front

Man, simple and brave, easily confiding,
Giving his all, glad of the sun's sweetness,
Heeding little of pitiful incompleteness,
Mending life with laughter and cheerful chiding,

Where is he? – I see him not, but I hear
Sounds, charged with nothing but death and maiming;
Earth and sky empty of all but flaming
Bursts, and shocks that stun the waiting ear;

Monsters roaring aloud with hideous vastness,
Nothing, Nothing, Nothing! And man that made them
Mightier far than himself, has stooped, and obeyed them,
Schooled his mind to endure its own aghastness,

Serving death, destruction, and things inert, –
He the soarer, free of heavens to roam in,
He whose heart has a world of light to home in,
Confounding day with darkness, flesh with dirt.

Oh, dear indeed the cause that so can prove him,
Pitilessly self-tested! If no cause beaconed
Beyond this chaos, better he bled unreckoned,
With his own monsters bellowing madness above him.

The Witnesses

I

Lads in the loose blue,
Crutched, with limping feet,
With bandaged arm, that roam
To-day the bustling street,

You humble us with your gaze,
Calm, confiding, clear;
You humble us with a smile
That says nothing but cheer.

Our souls are scarred with you!
Yet, though we suffered all
You have suffered, all were vain
To atone, or to recall

The robbed future, or build
The maimed body again
Whole, or ever efface
What men have done to men.

II

Each body of straight youth,
Strong, shapely, and marred,
Shines as out of a cloud
Of storm and splintered shard,

Of chaos, torture, blood,
Fire, thunder, and stench:
And the savage shattering noise
Of churned and shaken trench

Echoes through myriad hearts
In the dumb lands behind; –
Silent wailing, and bitter
Tears of the world's mind!

You stand upon each threshold
Without complaint. –What pen
Dares to write half the deeds
That men have done to men?

III
Must we be humbled more?
Peace, whose olive seems
A tree of hope and heaven,
Of answered prayers and dreams,

Peace has her own hid wounds;
She also grinds and maims.
And must we bear and share
Those old continued shames?

Not only the body's waste
But the mind's captivities –
Crippled, sore, and starved –
The ignorant victories

Of the visionless, who serve
No cause, and fight no foe!
Is a cruelty less sure
Because its ways are slow?

Now we have eyes to see.
Shall we not use them then?
These bright wounds witness
What men may do to men.

I am here, and you

I am here, and you;
The sun blesses us through
Leaves made of light.
The air is in your hair;
You hold a flower.

O worlds, that roll through night,
O Time, O terrible year,
Where surges of fury and fear
Rave, to us you gave
This island-hour.

Hunger

I come among the peoples like a shadow.
I sit down by each man's side.

None sees me, but they look on one another,
And know that I am there.

My silence is like the silence of the tide
That buries the playground of children;

Like the deepening of frost in the slow night,
When birds are dead in the morning.

Armies trample, invade, destroy,
With guns roaring from earth and air.

I am more terrible than armies,
I am more feared than the cannon.

Kings and chancellors give commands;
I give no command to any;

But I am listened to more than kings
And more than passionate orators.

I unswear words, and undo deeds.
Naked things know me.

I am first and last to be felt of the living.
I am Hunger.

Ypres

She was a city of patience; of proud name,
Dimmed by neglecting Time; of beauty and loss;
Of acquiescence in the creeping moss.
But on a sudden fierce destruction came
Tigerishly pouncing: thunderbolt and flame
Showered on her streets, to shatter them and toss
Her ancient towers to ashes. Riven across,
She rose, dead, into never-dying fame.

White against heavens of storm, a ghost, she is known
To the world's ends. The myriads of the brave
Sleep round her. Desolately glorified,
She, moon-like, draws her own far-moving tide
Of sorrow and memory; toward her, each alone,
Glide the dark Dreams that seek an English grave.

The Arras Road

I
The early night falls on the plain
In cloud and desolating rain.
I see no more, but feel around
The ruined earth, the wounded ground.

There in the dark, on either side
The road, are all the brave who died.
I think not on the battles won;
I think on those whose day is done.

Heaped mud, blear pools, old rusted wire,
Cover their youth and young desire.
Near me they sleep, and they to me
Are dearer than their victory.

II
Where now are they who once had peace
Here, and the fruitful tilth's increase?
Shattered is all their hands had made,
And the orchards where their children played.

But night, that brings the darkness, brings
The heart back to its dearest things.
I feel old footsteps plodding slow
On ways that they were used to know.

And from my own land, past the strait,
From homes that no more news await,
Absenting thoughts come hither flying
To the unknown earth where Love is lying.

There are no stars to-night, but who
Knows what far eyes of lovers true
In star-like vigil, each alone
Are watching now above their own?

III
England and France unconscious tryst
Keep in this void of shadowy mist
By phantom Vimy, and mounds that tell
Of ghostliness that was Gavrelle.

The rain comes wildly down to drench
Disfeatured ridge, deserted trench.
Guns in the night, far, far away
Thud on the front beyond Cambrai.

But here the night is holy, and here
I will remember, and draw near,
And for a space, till night be sped,
Be with the beauty of the dead.

An Incident at Cambrai

In a by-street, blocked with rubble
And any-way-tumbled stones,
Between the upstanding house-fronts'
Naked and scorched bones,

Chinese workmen were clearing
The ruins, dusty and arid.
Dust whitened the motley coats,
Where each his burden carried.

Silent they glided, all
Save one, who passed me by
With berry-brown high-boned cheeks
And strange Eastern eye.

And he sang in his outland tongue
Among those ruins drear
A high, sad, half-choked ditty
That no one heeded to hear.

Was it love, was it grief, that made
For long-dead lips that song?
The desolation of Han
Or the Never-Ending Wrong?

The Rising Sun and the Setting,
They have seen this all as a scroll
Blood-smeared, that the endless years
For the fame of men unroll.

It was come from the ends of the earth
And of Time in his ruin gray,
That song, the one human sound
In the silence of Cambrai.

Wingless Victory

I

Victory! Was that proud word once so dear?
Are difficulty, patience, effort hard
As danger's edge, disputing yard by yard
The adversary without and the mind's fear,
Are these our only angels? friends austere
That find our hidden greatness out, and guard
From the weak hour's betrayal faith unmarred!
For look! how we seem fall'n from what we were.

Worms feed upon the bodies of the brave
Who bled for us: but we bewildered see
Viler worms gnaw the things they died to save.
Old clouds of doubt and weariness oppress.
Happy the dead, we cry, not now to be
In the day of this dissolving littleness!

II

O you dear Dead, pardon! For not resigned,
We see, though humbled, half our purpose bent
And our hope blurred, like men in banishment.
Giants amid a blank mist groping blind,
The nations ache. And old greeds unconfined
Possess men, sick at battle's blood hot-spent
Yet sleek and busy and righteously content
To wage war, safe and secret, on their kind.

If all were simple as the way of hate!
But we must reap where others sowed the seed
In time long past, of folly and pride and greed;
Confused with names, idols and polities;
Though over all earth, where we think a State,
There are but men and women; only these.

III

Victory, winged, has flown far off again.
She is in the soul, she travels with the light.
We see her on the distant mountain height
Desired, but she has left us in the plain,
Left us awhile, to chafe and to complain,
Yet keep our wills, in this dark time's despite,
Like those that went up to the horrible fight
Beneath their burdens, plodding in the rain.

Courage! The same stuff that so greatly bore
And greatly did, is here, for gods to find,
And the dear human cause in the heart's core.
Be the task always harder than we know,
And victory further, yet in pain we grow.
The vision is before us, not behind.

Pain

Find me out a fortress, find
Such a mind within the mind
As can gather to its source
All of life's inveterate force,
Find the hard and secret cell
In my body's citadel,
Iron-ribbed from suck and drain
Of the clutching monster, Pain –
Pain, the formless alien will
That seeks me out, that strives to drill
Through shielding thought and barricade
Of all the strength my will has made;
That singles me and searches through
The sharp sense I am narrowed to;
And ever as the bond I strain
Thrusts me home to flesh again,
Estranging me from earth, to be
One fierce throb of identity!
Yet there's fibre in the mind
I shall find, I shall find,
To resist and to defy
All the world that is not I.

The Things that Grow

It was nothing but a little neglected garden,
Laurel-screened, and hushed in a hot stillness;
An old pear-tree, and flowers mingled with weeds.
Yet as I came to it all unawares, it seemed
Charged with mystery; and I stopped, intruding,
Fearful of hurting that so absorbed stillness.
For I was tingling with the wind's salty splendour,
And still my senses moved with the keel's buoyance
Out on the water, where strong light was shivered
Into a dance dazzling as drops of flame.
The rocking radiance and the winged sail's lifting
And the noise of the rush of the water left behind
Sang to my body of movement, victory, joy.
But here the light was asleep, and green, green
In a veined leaf it glowed among the shadows.
A hollyhock rose to the sun and bathed its flowers
Luminously clustered in the unmoving air;
A butterfly lazily winked its gorgeous wings;
Marigolds burned intently amid the grass;
The ripening pears hung each with a rounded shadow:
All beyond was drowned in the indolent blueness;
And at my feet, like a word of an unknown tongue,
Was the midnight-dark bloom of the delicate pansy.
Suddenly these things awed my heart, as if here
In perishing blossom and springing shoot were a power
Greater than shipwrecking winds and all wild waters.

Doing and Making

I am weary of doing and dating
The day with the thing to be done,
This painful self translating
To a language not my own.

Give me to fashion a thing;
Give me to shape and to mould;
I have found out the song I can sing,
I am happy, delivered, and bold.

The Wood's Entry

So old is the wood, so old,
Old as Fear.
Wrinkled roots; great stems; hushed leaves;
No sound near.

Shadows retreat into shadow,
Deepening, crossed.
Burning light singles a low leaf, a bough,
Far within, lost.

The Idols (excerpts)

On a starr'd, a still mid-night
Lost I halted, lost I gazed about.
Great shapes of trees branched black into the sky:
There was no way but wandered into doubt;
There was no light
In the uncertain desert of dim air
But such as told me of all that was not I, –
Of powers absorbed, intent, and active without sound,
That rooted in their unimagined might,
Over me there ignoring towered and spread.
Homeless in my humanity, and drowned
In a dark world, I listened, all aware;
And that world drew me.
The shadowy crossing of the boughs above my head
Enmeshed me as with undecipherable spells:
The silence laid invisible hands upon my heart,
And the Night knew me.

★

There is singing of brooks in the shadow, and high in a
       stainless
Solitude of the East
Ineffable colour ascends like a spirit awaking:
Slowly Earth is released.
It is dawn, it is dawn, the light is budding and breaking.

Earth is released, flowing out from the void of the
       darkness
Into body and bloom;
Flowing out from the nameless immensity, night, where
       she waited

Myriad forms to resume,
Gloriously moulded, as if in her freshness created.

The lineaments of the hills, serene in their order,
Arise, and the trees
With their motionless fountains of foliage, perfect in
        slumber;
And by lovely degrees
The blades of the grass re-appear, minute without
        number.
The rounded rock glistens and warms, where the water
        slips by it,
Familiar of old.
The tree stretches up to the air its intimate branches
Bathing in gold;
And the dew-dazzle colours in fire the lichen it blanches.

Each is seen in its beauty of difference, deeply
        companioned,
Leaf, root, and the stone,
And drawn by the light from their dream in earth's
        prison, emerging
Distinct in their own
Form, from the formless a million natures are urging.

I see them, I know them, I name them, I share in their
        being;
I am not betrayed:
I feel in my fibre the touch of a spirit that knows me;
For this was I made;
In a world of delight and of wonder my senses enclose me.

From Goethe

Peace is perfect over
All the hills.
Scarce wilt thou discover
A breath, so still's
Every tree.
The woods are silent; birds have hushed their song.
Wait but thou; ere long
Peace comes to thee.

The Second War

Anniversary
(November 11)

I

Thunder in the night! Vague, ghostly, remote
It rolls. The world sleeps. Suddenly splitting the air,
Stumbles a crash: and a million sleepers awake,
Each in his silence menaced, and all aware.

The aroused and secret spirit in each listens,
Companioned by an invisible listening host,
And sees the blackness gashed with quaking light,
Surrendered then to sounds of a world lost

In a heart-shaking convulsion of senseless force,
Wandering and warring blasts of a monstrous breath,
Legendary Chaos throned in heaven and dealing
Purposeless darts, and the air vivid with death.

But we, we are men, that walk upright in the sun,
That judge, question, remember, and foresee.
What have we to do with blind demons of air?
We choose and act; aim, reason, and are free.

Thunder in the night! As stupefying and sudden,
The stumbling crash of the nations into flame
Woke us aghast! We looked, we heard; we knew
That from us men the inhuman chaos came.

From reason, frenzy; from knowledge, blindness; from
        pity,
Cruelty! Trapped in Necessity's iron net,
To be free, to be free, we battled, and hoped the dawn,

Nor counted cost, if flesh could pay the debt.
O beauty broken! O glory of thought exiled!
O flowers in a furnace tossed! O joy defaced!
O sense and soul grown used in the fire, assenting
To brute futility, torture, and waste, waste!

The Spirit of Man in anguish amid the cloud
And the antiphons of thunder, and earth upheaved,
Beheld amazed the deeds of its body, and rose
In them to a splendour strange and unconceived.

II
They who simply heard the call of their own land,
The fields, the hills, the hamlets that they knew,
Hurt and in peril, and questioned not, but went,
To a fibre deep in the very body true;

They who high in hope of youth and flame of faith
Streamed to the storm with a beating heart of pride
Because that threat towered black against the sun,
Who fell, and made a radiance where they died;

They who would not for their soul's sake stand apart,
They who took upon themselves the world's red stain,
Who saw, who loathed, yet would not bear to watch
The struggle of others in unpartner'd pain;

They who still, when the mind sickened, and faith
        darkened,
And falsehood clung as the mud clung, and the cloud
Confused, and horror gnawed, endured to death,
Still seeing the star to which their course was vowed;

Them we name over, them we recall to-day,
Whose dear bodies in foreign earth are laid.
Ours is the light to breathe, and a world to mould:
But over them all is sleep; their hands are stayed.

Have we only remembering tears, and flowers to strew?
They are crying to us with the cry of the unfulfilled,
Like the earth aching for spring, when frosts are late.
Are we the answer? Or shall they twice be killed?

Their pain is upon us, pain of hope imperilled.
They are crying to us with the spirit's untold desires.
Heart, brain, and hand, the will and the vision – all,
And more than all, the Cause of Man requires.

We stumble and plod; by little and little we gain.
Old folly tempts, old habit about us twines.
But to-day our eyes are lifted, and hearts with them;
And near, as the stillness falls, the Vision shines.

In Hospital

I

Nothing of itself is in the still'd mind, only
A still submission to each exterior image,
Still as a pool, accepting trees and sky,

A candid mirror that never a breath disturbs
Nor drifted leaf, – as if of a single substance
With every shape and colour that it encloses, –

When, alone and lost in the morning's white silence,
Drowsily drowsing eyes, empty of thought,
Accept the blank breadth of the opposite wall.

Lying in my bed, motionless, hardly emerged
From clouds of sleep, – a solitary cloud
Is not more vague in the placeless blue of ether

Than I, with unapportioned and unadjusted
Senses, that put off trouble of understanding,
Even the stirring of wonder, and acquiesce.

The early light brims over the filled silence.
Memory stirs not a wave or a shadow within me.
Only the wall is the world; there stops my sight.

II

If he should bend his bow, that great Archer
There before me, if tautened and all erect
Slowly he should draw the arrow back to his ear,

Suddenly I should see the curve of his tense body
Alter, and O at the leap of the sighted arrow
The arms descend, shoulder and hip relax.

But hidden in his face, hidden the bow behind him.
I see the square of the buckle that clasps embossed
The belt girding the slenderness of his loins,

The smooth and idle energy of his arms,
And under the mould of breast and flank I feel
The invisible veins and warm blood pulsing through
        them.

But why is his face hidden? And why does my heart
Beat with a fear that he may be all disclosed
Terrible in calm, terrible in beauty and power?

For his eyes must surely be filled with the far mountains,
Rivers and great plains be his eyes' possession;
And full in the centre of his concentred vision

Stands his victim, he who is soon to be stricken,
Soon to fall, with the arrow pouncing upon him,
The arrow that carries the light and scorn of his eyes.

Why do you hide your face, glorious Archer?
If I could see you, then though the arrow pierced me
Gazing upon you, it were a glory to fall.

Will you at last, seizing the bow, bend it?
Now, as I gaze? A thrilling of fear rushes
Blind in my veins: fear? is it fear, or hope?

As if all my gaze were fixt on a drop of water
Suspended, about to fall and still not falling,
A liquid jewel of slowly increasing splendour

As the rain retreats and the shadow of cloud is lifted

And all light comes to enclose itself in the circle
Of a single drop, so is this suspended moment.

III

The stillness moves. Tripping of feet; shadows;
Voices. The hospital wakes to its ritual round.
The moment breaks; the drop, the bright drop falls.

A sponge has prest its coldness over my spirit.
Shape and colour abandon their apparition,
Subside into place in the order of usual things.

And another mind returns with the day's returning,
Weaving its soft invisible meshes around me.
This is the daylight, bald on the plain wall.

Cracks in the paint, a trickle of random lines,
A trailing scrawl that a child might trace with a stick
As he runs idly about the ebb-tide sands –

Is it out of these I supposed a towering image
There on the blankness? Are you gone, my Archer,
You who were living more than the millions waking?

No, you are there still! It was I released you
Out of the secret world wherein you are hidden.
You are there, there; and the arrow is flying, flying....

And yet patient, as if nothing were endangered,
We do small things and keep the little commandments, –
We and our doings a scribble upon the wall.

August Afternoon

Thump of a horse's hoof behind the hedge;
Long stripes of shadow, and green flame in the grass
Between them; discrowned, glaucous poppy-pods
On their tall stalks; a rose
With its great thorns blood-red in the slant light;
Round apples swelling on the apple-boughs: –
Over these, over the rich quiet, comes
Out of no-where a 'plane in the high blue
Driving its angry furrow across the sky,
Outstrips the slow clouds, throbs, an urgent roar,
Right overhead, and fiercely vanishes.
  The quiet has become strange. Like from pools
A noiseless water issuing, memories,
Surmises, apprehensions, traceless thoughts,
Glide with brief visions on the mind, drifting
From shadow into shadow; and then a pang
Sudden as when a meteor scars the night:
See where Christ's blood streams in the firmament!
Dead faces of the young, that see nothing...
The unknown wounds, everywhere, everywhere...
  And then from the inner to the outer sense
Returns the sun-warm quiet on the grass,
The poppy charged with sleep, the red, red thorns,
The stamping of the horse behind the hedge,
The strong slow patience of the living earth
And the apple ripening on the apple-tree
Almost as if I felt it in my flesh.

The North Star

I was contented with the warm silence,
Sitting by the fire, book on knee;
And fancy uncentred, afloat and astray,
Idled from thought to thought
Like a child picking flowers and dropping them
In a meadow at play.
I was contented with the kind silence,
When there invaded me –
Not a sound, no, there was no sound,
But awareness of a menace
Creeping up round
The little island of my mind;
A creeping up of gradual waves out of a sea,
With storm coming behind;
Wave on pale wave, smile on inhuman smile,
Driven on by the black force of alien will
To drown my world, to be the burial
Of joy, beauty, and all
That seemed impossible to kill;
Even the secret home that hope inherited.
I sat in an unreal room alone.
Befriending and familiar shapes were gone:
And I was seized with dread.

Then I became restless,
As if in bonds that must at any cost be burst.
The very peace seemed to oppress:
I was imprisoned and athirst,
And rose, and crossed the floor,
Craving to front the naked outer night.
At the opened door
Stood a thin mist, ghostly and motionless.

Smell of the leaves rotting
Breathed through a cold vapour
Bitter to the nostril.
My feet stumbled;
In my heart was a cry:
O for some single point of certitude!
I lifted up my face, and saw the sky.

There where I stood
Low mist clung to the earth.
But above, pale and diminished,
Only the larger lights pierced the dim air.
I faced the North.
And far and faint over a shadowy pine
That rose out of the mist
I saw the North Star shine.

I remembered sailors of old
For whom unclouded night
Was stretched above the dark Mediterranean,
A blue tapestry pricked with powdery gold,
Where legendary presences shone bright,
Each with a memory and a name;
And under the luminous maze
Steering by the North Star
Ships to their harbour came.

And now through thick silence
On the stifled fog-possessed Atlantic
I was hearing, distant or near,
Muffled answer of horn to horn,
The rocking clang of the buoy-bell, –
Sound crossing sound, to warn
Steamers, that on their blinded motion still

Unfaltering over seas invisible
Held to a silent clue
Because with the assurance of that star
The needle points them true.

There was a voice whispered:
Ascend, ascend!
Out of the earthy vapour, out
Of the invading doubt,
Into deliverance, into bare
Heights of unmeasured air.

Utterly stilled I stood,
Climbing in dizzying thought without an end
To that magnetic light,
That affirmation of old certitude.
And pinnacled alone in the vast night
My thought was there.

Oh, earth is gone.
My earth is lost.
North Star, North Star,
Dost thou fail me?
Thou art not what thou wast,
And all I was is taken from my mind:
For there is neither path nor direction
For any thought to find,
No North, nor South, nor East, nor West,
But homelessness suspended out of time,
Where I had sought to climb.
North Star, it was no shroud
Of mist, nor glory of overflowing sun;
It was no blotting curtain of blank cloud,
But a thought in the mind that deposed thee.

Down, down I sink:
Earth again holds me.
Again, North Star, I see thee shine.
But from the naked night I will not shrink;
And privately I take
A courage for thy sake,
Because thou hast thy place and I have mine;
Because I still need thee;
Because thou need'st not me.

Sowing Seed

As my hand dropt a seed
In the dibbled mould
And my mind hurried onward
To picture the miracle
June should unfold,

On a sudden before me
Hanging its head,
With black petals
Rotting and tainted,
Stood a flower, dead;

As if all the world's hope
Were rotting there,
A thing to weep for,
Ripe for burial,
Veined with despair.
Yet I cannot prevent
My ignorant heart
From trust that is deeper
Than fear can fathom
Or hope desert.

The small twy-bladed
Shoot will thrust
To brave all hazards.
The seed is sown
And in Earth I trust.

The Trembling Tree

On greenest grass the lace of lights
Beneath the shadowing tree
Trembles, as when eyes more than lips
Are smiling silently.

Its motion all but motionless
Is like a dancer's feet
Half-stirred, half-stilled, ere music throb
To float them on its beat.

Is it a music ears can hear?
Or in a world so jarred
With inward wrong, is it a sound
Too happy to be heard?

O tell me, tell me! Could I slip
The time's perversity,
There would be music in the air
And I that trembling tree.

A spirit smiling to itself
Seems in those leaves to live;
And for a moment, lost in it,
I can this world forgive.

There is Still Splendour

I

O when will life taste clean again? For the air
Is fouled: the world sees, hears; and each day brings
Vile fume that would corrupt eternal things,
Were they corruptible. Harsh trumpets blare
Victory over the defenceless; there
Beauty and compassion, all that loves the light,
Is outcast; thousands in a homeless night
Climb misery's blind paths to the peak, Despair.
  Not only martyr'd flesh, but the mind bleeds.
There's nothing left to call inhuman, so
Defaced is man's name by the things men do.
O worse, yet worse, if the world, seeing this,
The hideous spawn of misbegotten creeds,
Grow used, drugged, deadened, and accept the abyss.

II

There is still splendour: the sea tells of it
From far shores, and where murder's made to lurk
In the clean waters; there, men go to work
Simply, upon their daily business, knit
Together in one cause; they think no whit
Of glory; enough that they are men. To those
Who live by terror, calmly they oppose
What wills, dares, and despises to submit.
  And the air tells of it: out of the eye's ken
Wings range and soar, a symbol of the free,
In the same cause, outspeeding the swift wind.
Millions of spirits bear them company.
This is the splendour in the souls of men
Which flames against that treason to mankind.

English Earth

As over English earth I gaze,
Bare down, deep lane, and coppice-crowned
Green hill, and distance lost in blue
Horizon of this homely ground,

A light that glows as from within
Seems glorifying leaf and grass
And every simple wayside flower
That knows not how to say Alas!

O Light, by which we live and move,
Shine through us now, one living whole
With dear earth! Arm us from within
For this last Battle of the Soul!

History

Time has stored all, but keeps his chronicle
In secret, beyond all our probe or gauge.
There flows the human story, vast and full;
And here a muddy trickle smears the page.

The things our hearts remember make a sound
So faint; so loud the menace and applause.
The gleaners come, with eyes upon the ground
After Oblivion's harvest, picking straws.

What is man, if this only has told his tale,
For whom ruin and blunder mark the years,
Whom continent-shadowing conquerors regale
To surfeiting, with glory of blood and tears?

He flaunts his folly and woe in a proud dress:
But writes no history of his happiness.

Stray Seed

A far look in absorbed eyes, unaware
Of what some gazer thrills to gather there;
Happy voice, singing to itself apart,
That pulses new blood through a listener's heart;
Bowed fortitude; and in an hour of dread
The scorn of all odds in a proud young head:
These are themselves, and being but what they are,
Of others' praise or pity have no care;
Yet still are magnets to an unknown need.
Invisible as the wind, sowing stray seed,
Life breathes on life, ignorant what it brings,
And spirit touches spirit on the strings
Where music is; courage from courage glows;
Shy powers in secret to themselves unclose;
And unbefriended hope in the cold dark
Nursing its patient solitary spark
Among the ashes of a world to-day
Will be to-morrow kindled far away
In young bosoms. O we have failed and failed
And never known if we or the world ailed,
Clouded and thwarted; yet perhaps the best
Of all we have done and dreamed of lives unguessed.

When I am only I

When I am only I,
The secret battle-ground
Of world and will, wherein
Self is so strictly bound,

Then am I condemned;
Then can I understand
The heart crumbling to dust
And the eyes stopt with sand.

But when, self fallen asleep,
Quickens through all my veins
The entrancing light, and stream
The rivers and the rains,

Though to the wondrous earth
The tendril senses cling
And amid living leaves
I, as a bird, sing.

The breath comes of a world
Beyond all human moan.
There I am lost, and there
I am come into mine own.

The Junipers

Gray the slow sky darkens
Over the downland track
Where the long valley closes
Under a smooth hill's back.

The slope is darkly sprinkled
With ancient junipers,
Each a small, secret tree:
There not a breath stirs.

I fear those waiting shapes
Of wry, blue-berried wood.
They make a twilight in my mind,
As if they drained my blood,

As if a spirit were prisoned
Within each writhen stem,
And no one knows their kindred
Nor what frustrated them.

Along the empty valley
Like a ghost go I;
My footsteps and my beating heart
Nothing signify,

Lost into nameless ages
That come, slow cloud on cloud,
From history's beginning
And all the future shroud.

When All the World is Hidden

When all the world is hidden
And there is only you,
When bosom beats to bosom
As if the heart broke through,

O never speech nor language
Song nor music told
The wonder more than all the world
That in my arms I hold.

Day is a dream abolished,
Sweet madness only true.
The night is burning beauty
Where there is only you.

Autumn Song

All is wild with change,
Large the yellow leaves
Hang, so frail and few.
Now they go, they too
Flutter, lifted, lying,
Everywhither strewn.
All is wild with change.

Nothing shrinks or grieves.
There's no time for sighing.
Night comes fast on noon,
Dawn treads after soon;
Days are springing, dying,
We with them are flying.
All is wild with change.

Lovers

Stars beyond number or imagination
Silent in the sky;
Shadowy valleys and dark woods over them,
Still, without a sigh;
A house, lost in vastness and in silence,
With no house nigh;
A room apart, with not a whisper in it
As the hours steal by:
Sleeping in our star-surrounded darkness,
You and I.

The Way Home

Many dreams I have dreamed
That are all now gone.
The world, mirrored in a dark pool,
How unearthly it shone!

But now I have comfort
From the things that are,
Nor shrink too ashamed from the self
That to self is bare.

More than soft clouds of leaf
I like the stark form
Of the tree standing up without mask
In stillness and storm,

Poverty in the grain,
Warp, gnarl, exposed,
Nothing of nature's fault or the years'
Slow injury glozed.

From the thing that is
My comfort is come.
Wind washes the plain road:
This is the way home.

The Burning of the Leaves

Five Poems

I

Now is the time for the burning of the leaves.
They go to the fire; the nostril pricks with smoke
Wandering slowly into a weeping mist.
Brittle and blotched, ragged and rotten sheaves!
A flame seizes the smouldering ruin and bites
On stubborn stalks that crackle as they resist.

The last hollyhock's fallen tower is dust;
All the spices of June are a bitter reek,
All the extravagant riches spent and mean.
All burns! The reddest rose is a ghost;
Sparks whirl up, to expire in the mist: the wild
Fingers of fire are making corruption clean.

Now is the time for stripping the spirit bare,
Time for the burning of days ended and done,
Idle solace of things that have gone before:
Rootless hope and fruitless desire are there;
Let them go to the fire, with never a look behind.
The world that was ours is a world that is ours no more.

They will come again, the leaf and the flower, to arise
From squalor of rottenness into the old splendour,
And magical scents to a wondering memory bring;
The same glory, to shine upon different eyes.
Earth cares for her own ruins, naught for ours.
Nothing is certain, only the certain spring.

II
Never was anything so deserted
As this dim theatre
Now, when in passive grayness the remote
Morning is here,
Daunting the wintry glitter of the pale,
Half-lit chandelier.

Never was anything disenchanted
As this silence!
Gleams of soiled gilding on curved balconies
Empty; immense
Dead crimson curtain, tasselled with its old
And staled pretence.

Nothing is heard but a shuffling and knocking
Of mop and mat,
Where dustily two charwomen exchange
Leisurely chat.
Stretching and settling to voluptuous sleep
Curls a cat.

The voices are gone, the voices
That laughed and cried.
It is as if the whole marvel of the world
Had blankly died,
Exposed, inert as a drowned body left
By the ebb of the tide.

Beautiful as water, beautiful as fire,
The voices came,
Made the eyes to open and the ears to hear,
The hand to lie intent and motionless,
The heart to flame,

The radiance of reality was there,
Splendour and shame.

Slowly an arm dropped, and an empire fell.
We saw, we knew.
A head was lifted, and a soul was freed.
Abysses opened into heaven and hell.
We heard, we drew
Into our thrilled veins courage of the truth
That searched us through.

But the voices are all departed,
The vision dull.
Daylight disconsolately enters
Only to annul.
The vast space is hollow and empty
As a skull.

III

Cold springs among black ruins? Who shall say
Whither or whence they stream?
If it could be that such translated light
As comes about a dreamer when he dreams –
And he believes with a belief intense
What morning will deride – if such a light
Of neither night nor day
Nor moon nor sun
Shone here, it would accord with what it broods upon, –
Disjected fragments of magnificence!
A loneliness of light, without a sound,
Is shattered on wrecked tower and purpled wall
(Fire has been here!)
On arch and pillar and entablature,
As if arrested in the act to fall.

Where a home was, is a misshapen mound
Beneath nude rafters. Still,
Fluent and fresh and pure,
At their own will
Amid this lunar desolation glide
Those living springs, with interrupted gleam,
As if nothing had died:
But who will drink of them?

Stooping and feeble, leaning on a stick,
An old man with his vague feet stirs the dust,
Searching a strange world for he knows not what
Among haphazard stone and crumbled brick.
He cannot adjust
What his eyes see to memory's golden land,
Shut off by the iron curtain of to-day:
The past is all the present he has got.
Now, as he bends to peer
Into the rubble, he picks up in his hand
(Death has been here!)
Something defaced, naked and bruised: a doll,
A child's doll, blankly smiling with wide eyes
And oh, how human in its helplessness!
Pondered in weak fingers
He holds it puzzled: wondering, where is she
The small mother
Whose pleasure was to clothe it and caress,
Who hugged it with a motherhood foreknown,
Who ran to comfort its imagined cries
And gave it pretty sorrows for its own?
No one replies.

IV

Beautiful, wearied head
Leant back against the arm upthrown behind,
Why are your eyes closed? Is it that they fear
Sight of these vast horizons shuddering red
And drawing near and near?
God-like shape, would you be blind
Rather than see the young leaves dropping dead
All round you in foul blasts of scorching wind,
As if the world, O disinherited,
That your own spirit willed
Since upon earth laughter and grief began
Should only in final mockery rebuild
A palace for the proudest ruin, Man?

Or are those eyes closed for the inward eye
To see, beyond the tortures of to-day,
The hills of hope, serene in liquid light
Of reappearing sky –
This black fume and miasma rolled away?
Yet oh how far thought speeds the onward sight!
The unforeshortened vision opens vast.
Hill beyond hill, year upon year amassed,
Age beyond age and still the hills ascend,
Height superseding height,
Though each had seemed (but only seemed) the last,
And still appears no end,
No end, but all an upward path to climb,
To conquer – at what cost!
Labouring on, to be lost
On the mountains of Time.

What are they burning, what are they burning,
Heaping and burning in a thunder-gloom?

Rubbish of the old world, dead things, merely names,
Truth, justice, love, beauty, the human smile,
All flung to the flames!
They are raging to destroy, but first defile;
Maddened, because no furnace will consume
What lives, still lives, impassioned to create.
Ah, your eyes open: open, and dilate.
Transfigured, you behold
The python that was coiled about your feet,
Muscle on muscle, in slow malignant fold,
Tauten and tower, impending opposite, –
A fury of greed, an ecstasy of hate,
Concentred in the small and angry eye.
Your hand leaps out in the action to defy,
And grips the unclean throat, to strangle it.

V

From shadow to shadow the waters are gliding, are gone,
They mirror the ruins a moment, the wounds and the void;
But theirs is the sweetness of silence in places apart:
They retain not a stain, in a moment they shine as they
            shone,
They stay not for bound or for bar, they have found
            out a way
Far from the gnawing of greed and the envious heart.

The freshness of leaves is from them, and the springing
            of grass,
The juice of the apple, the rustle of ripening corn;
They know not the lust of destruction, the frenzy of spite;
They give and pervade, and possess not, but silently pass;
They perish not, though they be broken; continuing
            streams,
The same in the cloud and the glory, the night and the light.

High over the Battling Street

High over the battling street
I watch the wind blow
In frenzy tearing the plane trees
That are tossing below.

The high balcony's railing
Casts a shadow unstirred:
Of this mad torment of air
The sun has not heard.

Winter Sunrise

It is early morning within this room; without,
Dark and damp; without and within, stillness
Waiting for day: not a sound but a listening air.

Yellow jasmine, delicate on stiff branches
Stands in a Tuscan pot to delight the eye
In spare December's patient nakedness.

Suddenly, softly, as if at a breath breathed
On the pale wall, a magical apparition,
The shadow of the jasmine, branch and blossom!

It was not there, it is there, in a perfect image;
And all is changed. It is like a memory lost
Returning without a reason into the mind;

And it seems to me that the beauty of the shadow
Is more beautiful than the flower; a strange beauty,
Pencilled and silently deepening to distinctness.

As a memory stealing out of the mind's slumber,
A memory floating up from a dark water,
Can be more beautiful than the thing remembered.

I turn to the window, and out of a low cloud
Is a brimming-over of brightness; dazzling the eye
With levelled brilliance, fiery-fresh, the Sun.

As in absent thought with dreaming eyes I gaze
On sudden shadows gliding across the rime
A vision comes before me in utter silence

The earth is moving, the earth is rolling over
  All that is usual all that goes unquestioned
  is taken from me
  wider, wider the doors of vision are opening

Horizon opening into unguessed horizons
And I with the earth am moving into the light
  The earth is moving, the earth is rolling over
  into the light   long, long
  shadows of trees run out
              are running across the grass.

With frosty plains, mountains and curving coasts
Cities and rivers, forests, burning deserts,
Seas and the sprinkled islands, passing, passing,
But all transparent! Under the generous earth
The careless waters, I see the original fires
Leaping in spasms, seeking to burst their prison
And I remember that human eyes have seen
Solid earth yawn and cities shaken to fragments
Ocean torn to the bottom and great ships swallowed,

Now more terrible than those blind convulsions
Are men at war; on land, on the seas, in the air,
War, war in the brain, in the obstinate will
              war in the brain, war in the will, war
No refuge or hiding place anywhere for the mind

And now I hear everywhere sound of battle
The seekers after destruction, there is no refuge
Death, death, death on the earth, in the sea, in the air
  Yet oh, it is a single soul always in the midst
Each is a single soul.

           O it cannot be, yet it is

Let me not be so stunned that I cannot feel . . .
Imagination is but a little cup
It can hold but a minim part
Can a little cup contain an ocean?

My dreaming eyes return
The flower of winter remembers its own season
And the beautiful shadow upon the pale wall
Is imperceptibly moving with ancient earth
Around the sun that timeless measures
                        sure and silent.

The Madness of Merlin

(excerpts from the verse play)

From Scene IX

TALIESIN: The singer knows but half of what he sings.
The heart stirs, the lips burn,
But the word is borne from afar
As wind bears a seed across the water,
And behold in the cranny of a rock
The shining of a flower!

> (*He takes his harp and sings*)
> I have sung of the red berry
> In white mist, and the stag
> Crashing through frozen reeds.
> I have sung of the prow carving
> Water into beauty
> In bays where the gulls cry;
> And flash of the blue spears
> When the chiefs toss their hair
> Rising proud by the hill.

But now I sing, for the heart is tender in me,
Of the compassionate gifts of God to mortals,
Beauty of the body, and the swiftness of the mind.

I see one who stands on a bare hill in the dawn.
The fading stars are about his head, and his arms
Stretch forth to salute the beginning of the light.

He opens his lips and his voice goes out singing,
With his voice he subdues the wild, the fierce creatures.
Among all sounds the voice of a man is the King.

He holds within his eyes the mirror of the world,
The feather upon the finch, the moss upon a stone,
The shadowy isles, the stedfast and the moving stars.

He brings the far things near, he weaves them into his
        thought.
His glances scatter seeds of courage and joy.
He sees as from a tower what was and is to be.

Two wonders I sing, and a third yet more wondrous.
Who created the smile on the lips of a man?
Who prepared the secret of the smile in his eyes?

Proud eyes of the falcon, gentle eyes of the hare,
Are prisoned in their gaze; only in man is the smile
That delivers from the world of hatred and fear.

Many words are as waves beating and broken in vain;
But the smile comes as a ship straight to its own harbour,
Bearing its riches with it, light to a dark house.

I sing of the smile which enters the hard heart,
Which overcomes sorrow with all understanding.
It is the last wisdom of sorrowing mortals.

MERLIN: Evil comes smiling, O Taliesin!

TALIESIN: All things suffer corruption
That have a mortal shape!

MERLIN: Give me the harp. Come, let me sing for you.
    (*He sings*)
    I will sing of the Wind,
    The invisible Wind
    That comes out of nothing,
    That cares for nothing.

Glorying in its leaves
Stands the tree at morning,
Sweet tryst of lovers. –
When darkness falls

Behold it fallen,
The wrenched roots lifted
Like hands despairing
Up to the storm.

'I have scourged the seas,'
Cries the Wind; 'I toss
The well-wrought keel
On the reef's strong jaws.

White bodies broken
Are there in the foam.
It is nothing to me
That make merry with death.

I hurl the dancing
Ice of the hail.
I smile not, but laugh
Loud through the sky.
Every-where, no-where,
I am and I am not.
Generations of mortals
Pass and are gone;

With bowed shoulders
They cough and shake,
They wither to dust:
I am young for ever.'

From Scene XIV

MERLIN: I see a plain, empty, wide as the whole world.
It has no end: for ages on ages
It stretches out, it leaves all thought behind.
The years pursue the years; like hurrying flames
They run, they are like wild torches, myriads
Streaming toward me. – No, they grow bigger and bigger,
They are men pursuing men; they populate the plain,
All on fire with anger, trampling and triumphing.
Hark, the dint of the hooves of their horses,
Multiplying each moment! Terrible horsemen!
Fiery nostrils of horses! Swifter and swifter
Riding and raging, a fury
Without beginning, without end.

Acknowledgements

The publisher is grateful to the Society of Authors as the Literary Representative of the Estate of Laurence Binyon.

Text sources for the poems: *The Four Years* (Elkin Matthews, 1919), *Collected Poems of Laurence Binyon* (two volumes, Macmillan, 1931), *The North Star and Other Poems* (Macmillan, 1941), *The Burning of the Leaves and Other Poems* (Macmillan, 1944) and *The Madness of Merlin* (Macmillan, 1947).

Binyon's first-hand account of British Red Cross and other volunteer aid activity in France during the First World War, *For Dauntless France*, was published by Hodder and Stoughton in 1918.

For details of Binyon's life I am greatly indebted to John Hatcher's biography, *Laurence Binyon: Poet, Scholar of East and West* (Clarendon Press, Oxford, 1995).

'In his master's moonlight' by Mick Imlah, a review of John Hatcher's biography, appeared in the *TLS*, July 1996.